Fr

An Anthology of Poems, Short Stories and Essays

The White Rose UK

Freedom!

An Anthology of Poems,

Short Stories and Essays

Composed by 36 Authors

Questioning Covid Restrictions and Lockdowns

The White Rose UK

ISBN-13: 979-8729434770

Published in May 2021, 1st edition

thewhiterose.uk

Contents

Preface

Who do you put at the beginning and end of an anthology? Let us begin with Stephen Gray's short story. The story is written from the perspective of a fictive child. After all, aren't the children the ones who will suffer the most from this 'health dictatorship' and who will have to live with the consequences that will follow these unprecedented times? Macy's work, a genuine child's voice, marks the end of the book. Her ending phrase: 'I would very much like to get to normal and stop all this nonsensical madness,' is a summary of what every other author in this book has expressed in their own words, in their unique way.

In *Freedom!* the reader will find a treasure of poems, short stories and essays from 36 authors, from all kinds of backgrounds. This book contains several literary pearls, but it is up to the reader to decide what counts as a pearl.

I would like to thank everyone who was involved in the making of *Freedom!*

Our voices have merged together into one strong voice, which is whispering, shouting, crying for freedom. May this book be a small, yet powerful contribution to a positive change in the world.

The White Rose UK

1

While We Weren't Looking

It always happened the same way: two taps against the window, very gently, just enough for you to realise a noise had been made, then a pause before the faintest of sounds could be heard again.

Always it came at night, frightening me when it did. Mother and Father were afraid too, once they recognized the sound as something that wasn't right and shouldn't have been there. Although Father did his best to hide his fear, I could hear it in his voice when he put his finger to his mouth and whispered to us to come away from the windows. Masie, our little dog, would whimper and scurry away, joining us in the room farthest away from those windows, and whatever lay beyond that glass.

The first time I heard it, I couldn't be sure I'd heard anything at all, but then it came again the next night and I drew back the curtains slowly, just enough to peer into the black world beyond. I didn't know what I expected to see. There were no street lights anymore since the power cuts, but there was something there in the darkness, just at the edge of sight, shifting against the shadows; something that shouldn't have been there. At first my parents wouldn't listen, and put it down to a child's imagination. Before long, though, they would hear it too, as we sat in the candlelight of the dark new world.

I was eight years old when the news came that we would soon have to stay away from school. I was so happy, I hated school. They didn't know how long we would have to stay away, but I hoped it would be forever. They said there was something new and dangerous in the air that could spread. Soon the adults were told to stay at home too, and I was happy and hoped we could live like this always, just us three together with Masie, away from the responsibilities of work and school; but soon the problems began. Mum and Dad would argue about things I didn't understand. They feared the lights would go out and it might be difficult to get food. No one had work and so the world couldn't turn properly. Shops were closed and people couldn't go outside. Once a week the power would return briefly, and a broadcast from the government was transmitted into homes. The reassuring voice of the Prime Minister said that everything would be okay, and things would return to normal soon enough, but after a while my Father would simply laugh at these words and sink into his seat, a look of defeat in his eyes, which upset my Mother. I'd retreat into another room with Masie, hiding before my parents began arguing once more.

Sometimes cars would go past outside and I'd wonder where they were going. The roads were mostly empty now, and quiet. The only vehicles were food trucks delivering weekly parcels to the neighbourhood, although they never seemed to deliver quite enough, and often I felt hungry. One day after months locked inside, and after he'd seen yet another car drive quickly by, my Father grabbed his keys and ushered us out into our own car. As he pulled out of the drive, I was both afraid and excited at the same time. We weren't supposed to leave our homes, but I desperately wanted to see the world again, and was shocked by how silent everything had become. On the motorway, there were few other cars, but whenever we passed one, horns sounded in greeting. We were rebels too, and the other drivers seemed to like that we had disobeyed the rules. Soon, in the distance, we saw policemen dressed in strange uniforms, black with dark helmets and visors, blocking the road with vehicles and barriers. They carried guns and I feared what they might do. Some drivers argued, demanding to know why they couldn't travel further. They were not a threat to anyone, they reasoned, but the police did not listen and fired their guns into the air. Far in the distance, against the hills and the sky, I could tell that something was different. Subtle, just outside of my vision where I couldn't quite reach, something that shouldn't have been there. While we'd been locked away, the world had changed.

Within days, the Prime Minister made his address to the nation, telling of dissenters refusing to obey the rules. These foolish people, he said, were causing the danger to spread, meaning the lockdown would continue longer than expected. To counter this, a new drug had been invented which would help prevent further contamination, and already this was being administered across the country. Large black vehicles began appearing on the streets overnight. My parents were angry. 'What right do they have to do this without consent?' they demanded, and my Father would sneak out to talk with others he knew might also dissent. Some spoke of shadowy figures inside the black vehicles, hidden behind tinted windows. And then, finally, there were those whom we'd known before: neighbours and friends, all different somehow. Changed. I would see them from the upstairs window, shuffling along, not quite who they once were, and sometimes I cried at what I saw.

Early one morning, we got into the car and drove away from home, saying goodbye for the last time. We packed camping equipment and as much food and water as we could. On that day I saw other things that should not have been there: great buildings in the distance which were not present before, cold and forbidding, reaching up into the sky. Even my parents looked on in astonishment, eyes wide and mouths open. What had happened while we had been locked in our homes, and why? The world had changed, but whatever had caused it was no longer hiding away out of sight. It was here and it didn't care that we knew.

Getting away was difficult. Police asked for 'papers', forcing us to backtrack and reconsider our route. The sinister black vehicles sometimes followed, like hunters tracking their prey. We never once saw the drivers.

And here I am now, a grown man, my parents long gone, but I do have a family. Those, like my parents, who stood against what was happening around them as best they could with little access to information, and a hostile government taking its orders from Lord knows who... or what? Looking into the distance we can see how our world has changed. Strange new architecture dominates the landscape now. The youngest of us has no memory of how the world used to be, but they know we are free. We didn't suffer the fate of the trusting majority. I wonder now where those people are? What sort of life they have? And I think then of ourselves, our growing numbers as more arrive each day, looking for shelter amongst us here in the mountains and woods. All of them believing in the time that will come when all the pieces have been gathered; when we find out the extent of what has happened to us, and we begin to take back what is rightfully ours.

Stephen James Gray

2

I Will Not Wear a Mask Today

I will not wear a mask today.
Today or any other day.
I don't believe a word they say.

We never needed masks before.
But now they're vital? Are you sure?
I watch my country with dismay.

Our cancer patients left to die
While covid death tolls are a lie.
I will not wear a mask today.

The seconds trickle by like hours
So many dreams now withered flowers.
Our once blue skies are cloudy grey.

What's next? We all stand out of doors
And clap for 1984
Today and every other day?

We know the lives our parents led

But make our kids wear masks instead.
It's time to organise and pray.

Don't touch. Don't sing. Don't speak. Don't smile.
A life like this is not worthwhile.
I don't believe a word they say.

I don't believe a word they say
Today or any other day.
I will not wear a mask today.

JK

3

Simon's Acrostic Poem

Controlling us for almost a year
Orders from the PM so many adhere.
Rights as a human are vanishing fast
Obnoxious lies the media does blast!
Not sure if this virus is real anymore
All of our country under this martial law.

Vaccination For All, is the cry
Immunization is not needed, so why?
Rights as a human are vanishing fast
Under control are the masses to the last!
Suicide, domestic violence, addiction, depression all
     on the rise.

Why keep feeding us these covid lies?
Only three weeks to flatten the curve, was their
     guarantee
Enough is enough, I want to be free!
Stand up people please, it can't be just me!

Simon Holland, 38

[Find the three hidden words by reading the first let-
ter of each line.]

4

What If

Lying in the morning bath
Winter sky – oasis
White through the glass
Bells calling left-over christians to order
I thought:
What would happen if we believed [just suddenly and
    completely]
That death was no threat?

Shouted out through megaphones
From smart trucks with banners.
Men laughing and waving.
Hugging.

Come out of your houses!
Life will not end!
There is no fear!
There is no sickness!

Would the wars and fears continue inside our minds
Windows slammed

Tutting against the outbreak of peace?

Or would the world breathe more freely
Of an emptiness that is the beginning
Of all things?

Gillian Watt

5

When the Army Sings

I sensed a rat. 'Something isn't ringing quite true,' I suggested to a friend, 'and I'm going to do something about it.' She sniggered. 'Truth? But how are you going to find that out exactly? You and whose army – The Army of Truth?'

Despondent, I walked away. But then I thought to myself: 'That's actually quite a good idea, I think I'll do exactly that!'

Over four months ago the seed was planted, and I worked hard to expand The Army of Truth. The membership grew and grew and we were all delighted with the progress and our findings, as we all excavated and researched what we were learning.

We had to make sure that everything we were posting was factual and could be documented and verified accordingly as genuine and sincere.

I was the only member in the group with admin rights and even to this day I still am, because I created it and nurtured it from its inception. I was also fully responsible for its longevity and existence. Despite constant scrutiny from our Facebook friends with fact checker assistance, we marched onwards and upwards.

It has been thus far an arduous journey but one that has broadened my own perspective and redefined me as a person, and the lessons and education process I have experienced along the somewhat bumpy road, have been literally invaluable and will remain with me indefinitely.

We hit the mark of 1,000 members then two, three, four and then five thousand members, and with each member we had found a new miner, and the researching became much easier, as we worked collectively making our jigsaw pieces match to establish an element of clarity as to the bigger picture.

Today the The Army of Truth has an excess of 15,000 members and when one voice spoke back then it echoed and whispered to me, but now the whispers grow louder as our crowds muster. Together we can bang the drum of truth.

One day the truth will surface and if we are victorious and achieve our objective to recalibrate the scales of justice to bring a level of equilibrium back to conventional living.

But I do often wonder if only more people had whispered, this battle would have been easier. But irrespective of the outcome – win, lose or draw – we can all take comfort, knowledge and pride that we stood side by side and tried.

We didn't just lie down and accept the unacceptable. We refused the shackles and to be silenced because we have a voice, and whether you like it or not, we are going to sing our anthem.

Because The Army of Truth fight for you, not against you and the truth is, you never knew.

But for now we soldier on ...

Steve Roberts, 54

6

Healing by Keeping People at Bay

Tomorrow, they say
Comes a fresher new day.
Overthinking of what happened in the past
I've finally detached from the labels at last.
Forgiveness is key, for anyone seeking a happier,
        freeing experience.
Phenomenally, we pay for that energy in humanly re-
        silience.
Time and time again, you were intuitively right
That in the darkest of the darks, YOU! were the light.
Make your own way down the rabbit hole
But be careful of the informative moles...
Finally, when you come face to face with rabbit
He shares the secret knowledge of the world which
        we inhabit.
Time and space are an illusion of the game
Make a choice, there's no one else to blame.

Bradley Xander, 33

7

Dance the Freedom Dance

Come on, let's get together
If we unite then we can end this forever.
Hey you, just open your heart
We were never made to stay apart.

Hey child, I won't apologize
For they're the ones who told us lies.
I cannot go back on what I've found
Now I'm not afraid to stand my ground.

Let's dance, the freedom dance
We can't miss this one and only chance.
Let's not submit, and just ask why
People aren't living before they die.

Don't believe all you were told to perceive
This is a world of mask and make-believe.

Heather Judd, 30

8

The Show

Welcome to the show!

Come on in, come and join us, don't be afraid – you
will be entertained!

The script carefully constructed by the best in the
trade!

The incognito authors rubbing their hands exclaim
'What a success!'

The actors who play, the stage is theirs

The audience is vast and their cheer is loud

They applaud, they clap admiring the cast

Their wide-open eyes firmly following the plot.

The show continues

The audience is hooked

Fiction and reality have signed a pact

United they are strong and intact.

Unaware, the audience drowns deeper

Reaching the final stage of hypnotic trance.

No one has noticed

The show should have ended a long time ago.

The actors are tireless

They will keep playing

Impressive monologues filling the gullible minds.

Polished techniques, rehearsed scenes

They have charisma, the stage is grand

Glorious effects and a promised new world.

What happened to the audience?

Why aren't they leaving, it is well past midnight...

Performers keep dancing in costumes that are shining

Their singing euphonious and audience obedient.

Delighted grandmothers

Ecstatic grandfathers

Worshipping the skilled performers.

Mesmerised mothers and influenced fathers

Forgot their small children who are now crying

Craving for human touch

And a long lost smile

When they grow up

Lonely and puzzled with a void in their hearts

They will take their parents' ragged seats.

Despair will vanish, escapism will flourish.

The sun is now rising

The air is tempting and crisp but so out of fashion.

The day is awake and inviting

Its true beauty no longer desired

As the locked away audience

Eagerly awaits the thrills of next chapters.

Alex Stapaj

9

A New Minority

It seems recently that society has been conditioned to protect 'minorities' against discrimination. Firstly, of course society was conditioned to identify and label minorities before this discrimination could occur. I now find others label me a minority; not a linguistic or race minority. A minority opinionist. I don't feel very protected right now. If I were inclined to victimize myself, I would say that I am being discriminated against. In reality, I know that what others think of me is none of my business, but this leaves me curious.

I have an opinion. I was raised to believe that one's own opinion was a natural right.

In December (prior to the necessity of testing) I travelled to see my family that live in a different country to me. I visited. I stayed a while. I did not catch our reserved flight back as I did not feel the necessity for my children and I to take a test that was unjustifiably expensive and proven to be scientifically inaccurate and exploited beyond it's intended purpose. Plus, I didn't actually have the money because I no longer have a business or income, as like a majority, I was forced to close shop. I am staying with family and we keep ourselves to ourselves. I have not socialised with anyone outside my family for months. I go to the supermarket at the least busy times and run or walk everyday to stay sane. I respect the space of those I encounter. I say to people I pass in the street: 'Good morning! Beautiful day!' Mostly, I am ignored, and people step back or cross the road to avoid me, looking in amazement as if I just dropped in from another planet. The fundamental and essential essence of social being appears to be threatened with extinction.

Why am I a minority? Because I cannot wear a mask to cover my face. Am I obliged to explain myself or my reasoning? Is a religious minority obliged to provide reasoning? Am I selfish? No, not at all. Those that know me, know that I care. I care a lot. I love people and my working life has been based upon making people feel good about themselves and making the most of the fabulous assets we are given, to enjoy our living experience – our body, our health the ability to choose and think critically. Health incidentally, as defined by the WHO is:

> 'A state of complete physical, mental and social well-being and not merely the absence of disease or infirmity.'

It seems that the higher echelons of global establishments put in place to serve the people and tell the truth, have forgotten their own definitions.

The ego within me could claim that I am discriminated against most days. I am labelled selfish, a conspiracy theorist, an eco-warrior, a hippy, a yogi, a non-complier, a murderer even... and more derogatory terms. The last time I checked, my body belonged to me, I am the owner holding full allodial title. I have jurisdiction over my body and the right to deny anything that I believe causes me harm, anxiety or deprivation; the right to decide whether I allow penetration of any orifice for any purpose.

I will not impose my views on others. I will not have a vaccine. Indeed, some of my beloved family have already chosen to take the vaccine. It is their born-right to do so, as, their opinion is that it will protect them, and I most certainly respect that and love them regardless of their personal choices or opinion. If they are protected, I do not pose a danger to them, or anyone else who has chosen to protect themselves by making the same choice. Surely, that is the point of taking it, right, to protect oneself?

Because my labelled belief and opinion may fall within a minority populous; because I hear I am a 'minority'; because my choice is not compliant with the applied narrative or claimed majority, do I deserve to be vilified? Do I deserve to be denied of freedoms because of my choices to decline? Should I just conform? Should I be made to conform through force against my will?

My children and I have not returned to my home now for months. We have left everything but a suitcase, and the three of us share a bed and a bedroom because I decline to take a scientifically unreliable test to prove to others that I am healthy and to provide me with yet another label.

Currently this is a very long dark tunnel. I have optimism for light at the end of it, plenty in fact, but some days it wanes a little...

My background is science, specifically human biology and biochemistry. I have done my homework. I have reached my conclusions from an informed standpoint and I continually remain open minded and strive to learn more. With greater learning and understanding, opinions can, and are entitled to change.

I have researched the statistics at length. Anyone can. I wish more people did. However, it seems the one main thing I am lacking is... television. I don't watch one. Perhaps that is the dealbreaker? Perhaps many choose to believe the TV over doing their own research. I would appreciate it if any of my black, white, straight, gay, Christian, Muslim, Polish, Danish, European, American, friends would explain to me how my ego is not being discriminated against, and how I can remain entitled to exercise the rights I was born with.

I appreciate this may strike a chord with many. Thus, in the same way you can change the channel on your TV if you don't like the programme, you can switch me off as a 'friend'.

Sincere love to those that choose to claim their freedom. To live in fear of dying is not living.

Sheryl Squirrell

10

The Old Normal

What would happen if we were to let go of our fears
and all of the emotions that link to the past?
To stop reliving certain moments over and over?
Could we be free?
Free to focus on the daily ritual of life?
Do you see how it works?
The emotional state plays a role in a person's envir-
onment. The two are connected, they bounce off
one another constantly.
They have said that we are what we think about.
So, if our thoughts are mostly Fear, Shame and Re-
gret.
What sort of state is the reality outside our mind go-
ing to be in?
What will manifest from that state?
Maybe this is the key
To navigating the world
Of the lost.
If a mindset dictates the environment, it is then our
duty to focus on Truth, Love and Community.

It might be the only way that we can change this
world that consumes us all.

S. Carter

A British Ghost Story

'They say the British are finished.'

'The British? They cannot be finished. Not the British who fought at Trafalgar, Waterloo, North Africa, Italy, and in the Falklands, and who held out through the Blitz.'

'But they are. The whole nation.'

'But I lived and fought with them. They can't be finished. Rubbish man! Listen to them sing as they marched through the streets of London on their way to France, and in the subway-stations when their enemies were trying to wipe them out and break their spirit! Hark, man, can you not hear them singing in the pubs, in the village halls and praying in their churches when the whole of Europe was overrun? All those indomitable spirits, lifting their pints and their prayer books and singing 'We'll Meet Again' and 'Jerusalem'. Why, man, they'll never die.'

'Aye, but they're still gone.'

'But look what they did in the Battle of Britain and throughout the Blitz. You couldn't kill 'em. They flew, fought, took shelter, fought, prayed, regrouped, fought again; they never fell back except to lick their wounds, bury their dead, and then go farther forward again. They fought, fought, fought; they never yielded. And when the whole shooting match was all over, cannot you remember how they thronged round the Victoria Memorial in front of the Palace, and down The Mall? No people in the world could have crowded together in such good humour and sung and cheered as they did. And when the King, Queen and Mr Churchill appeared on the balcony and the bands played 'God Save the King', why, man, you never saw the King and Queen and the Prime Minister up there; you saw only the immense, innumerable crowd of Britons from the United Kingdom and from all over her Commonwealth of Nations, and you saw all they had done, and all that they were, and the sacrifices they had made, the courage they had shown. You saw their flags carried high, the Union Flag, and flags from the whole Commonwealth, and your eyes dampened, and involuntarily you shed a tear.'

'Aye, but they're still gone.' The nation lost its courage and faith and belief in freedom. People became fearful of risk, gave in to fear of pain, illness and death, and so became as driven cattle, afraid to live, except as slaves, in blind obedience of their omnipotent government.

'But that cannot have happened, man. One night, if you stay here, you'll see them come back out of the darkened cities and countryside. They'll be a bit grey in the face, but they'll be here alright. They'll still be advancing and singing; they'll bring their old and their sick and wounded with them, but they'll still come. Make no mistake. And they'll make Britain proud again, and make merry, and be light-hearted. And when they've beaten the tyrants who've tried to enslave them, they'll go back to their old ways. And they'll meet together and laugh, worship, drink and sing, and knowing that times have been tough, they'll dismiss them, forget them and speak to their children only of the brightness of the future. And when the children ask them what the covid crisis was all about, they will say, 'It was nothing.'

'Look, man, here they come now; I told you they couldn't die.'

We who were left peered into the night-mist.

'Who goes there?' shouted a soldier.

'Friend,' came back the reply.

'Advance, friend, and be recognised.'

But there came only the sound of the wind.

[With apologies to William Woodruff, author of 'Vessel of Sadness']

Leslie Fellows, 74

12

My Own Howl

Today's howl is gratitude for long lines of sleet like a
    wallpaper pattern outside my window.
Crisscrossed with childhood panes
Thick walls with tiny window seat sans cushion.

Howling at the weirdness in the morning dreaming of
    my sister
Daisy, in a yellow dress
Yellow daisy baggage, baggage somebody, carrying it
    but not me.
Waking remembering of evil in a documentary in the
    kitchen warm mouths open

The psychiatrists with their instruments
Torture – it works to stun pigs before slaughter
Why not people?

Down with eugenics, with racism fat and ugly.
Men who think that others like them
The piggy eyes, flabby noses, thin tight lips.
Fat buttocks sitting above us

Look down the Parson's nose.

Irony of the ugly deciding who is to be beautiful.

Down with stupidity and ignorance!
Down with men who say they are intelligent but only
    want power!
Down with everyday torture, tranquillising, and docil-
    ity!
Down with Book Depository and polite emails that
    explain nothing!
Down with fraudulent advertising!
Down with all the protective bars to keep capitalism
    safe!

Long Live the corporation they say
The King is dead! Long live The King!

Down with winter!
Down with cold feet and old shoes!
Down with ever-hungry cats!
Down! Down! Down with lies!

I woke this morning and remembered
I didn't know where to go in my bed up against a
    wall.
I am. We are.
We don't know how to move forward

We are stopped at every turn. Deep, deep, in the
      night of my just-awake mind, I dug
Past all the too-old-to-eat puffballs like severed
      dusty heads,
Past the putrid waste, the dark of despair or
      whatever you want to call it, and I found [by feel
      alone you understand]
Some jewels.
I dragged them through the sludge and the seaweed
      to the surface
I made my mind repeat them.
Sanskrit or Tibetan don't know which
Gobbledy gook
Or gooky gobble
Medicine Buddha.
This is how it is:

The end of suffering
The end of biggest suffering
The end of suffering is the King of everything.
It covers more than every ocean
I hold it forever in my heart.

Over and over like a dripping tap.
Not enough to clean it all

But drip, drip I remember faith, I remember light,
I remember the sun, I remember truth.

I get up and make a cup of tea.

Gillian Watt

13

Lost Youth

The insanity of a man knocked up with his kids all
day.

Fear, fear, fear.

No festival, no love, no touching.

Fear, fear, fear.

All day alone – fear, fear, fear.

Mustn't doubt the scientist, mustn't doubt them.

Mustn't doubt the life times repaying the money that
was never there.

Fear, fear, fear.

Mustn't doubt them, mustn't doubt them, they're experts didn't you know?

Didn't you know.

Blinded, blinded we stagger on, fear fear fear.

Our dreams in ruins – blame the virus! Blame the virus!

Do what they tell you to do, it's the responsible
thing!

Fear, fear, fear.

Speakers corner blocked off, cranks no more, meeting no more, fear fear fear.

I have something left... hatred and revenge for the
scientists and experts whose lies prevail.
It's better than fear, fear, fear!

Frankreich Rootin, 60

14

Sleep Now

All the magicians are up on the stage
And all of their secrets are being revealed.
Crumbling illusions and limited days
The liberty thieves are no longer concealed.

It's all there to see if we choose, right in front of our
        eyes
If we lift our heads for enough time to breathe in the
        truth.
If you think you're complete, then you'll fall off your
        seat and you'll cry
When you find your perception of freedom has
        crashed through the roof.

So, sleep now, but you won't see what's coming
        along
Sleep now and wake up when it's all gone wrong.
Sleep now, good night my little consumer
Sleep now, you'd better hold on to your sense of hu-
        mour.

Gregg Brown, 50

[I originally wrote this as a song in 2004, frustrated at the general apathy in society and I think it applies now, more than ever before.]

15

Building Back Better?

There is a vacancy in compassion and empathy within the human race and it has been engineered to be this way, through social engineering and mind control. That vacancy is being rapidly filled with steely reactions through deceptive distractions, fostering transhumanism agendas, creating the cyborg through mute compliance, initiating the singularity of artificial intelligence interconnecting to the neurological processes of human kind. We have reached the event horizon of the demise of humanity as we know it.

Anyone who complies to any governmental dictate has blood on their hands. You are sponsoring and promoting orchestrated famines and the genocide of billions, the destruction of human society and the entire natural world as we know it. The suffering of billions, the suicide of millions and the rape and torture of innocent victims, the list can go on but you get my point! The world is being signed up [by forced subscription – that reminds me of the BBC license people strangely pay for each year] to become transhuman [cyborgs].

It's not a vaccine, technically it's a method of geoengineering humans, updating human software shot after shot. It rewrites genetic code and uploads new data. Humans are merely the host agents being prepared for upgrade, 'fixed up' to fit into a 'New Normal' World Order. The singularity [fusion of body and machine]. The vaccine is just an excuse of a name because no one wants to be turned into mind-machines [well at least most don't]. They even tell us all that it won't cure the C virus [seasonal Influenza A and B strains, which is what this pathogen actually is]. It's nothing new, and never has there been a cure for the common cold.

Starvation, suicide, no work, no career, just more government bollocks about fake virus strains. Zero science, just very sloppy pseudo science [otherwise known as nonscience], 5G and vax genocide. Welcome to a cyborg future, transhumanism is the rule of the day [the singularity – mind and machine fused forever, altered and manipulated and controlled forever]. Crime in the home and on the streets is set to grow exponentially... all planned! And the NHS is waiting in empty hospitals and fake testing centres, go figure! Global populations for the majority are apathetically and misguidedly optimistic and lack incentives to act against it all because the masses have been spoon fed toxic words along with toxically engineered food, whilst breathing in the toxic air for so long that it is now not within their natural ability to say No! They simply shrug their slumped shoulders and shuffle along with the orders of the day, easier for them that way, and it can be clearly seen that a minority would rather experience exist-ence as autonomously as possible, and so the balance can be readdressed and the harm upon the people can be healed. It is better to share love and compassion than up-hold by demonstration examples of hate and dis-compas-sion, because the seeds we plant grow into the light, and if we promote and perpetuate the growth of bad seeds they dominate the light. There is always a balance and the bad will always exist but we can choose not to allow the neg-ative to dominate. When we feel our vulnerability we feel compassion and when we feel compassion we feel the sanctity of all existence.

Salena Shatki Radford, 56

What Is Freedom?

Freedom is running barefoot in the sand.

Freedom is having messy hair and feeling ok about it.

Freedom is hearing a creak on the stairs and knowing
Teddy will protect you.

Freedom is deliberately running into clean white
sheets hanging on the washing line.

Freedom is hearing the rain splashing on the roof,
feeling all snuggly under the duvet.

Freedom is being in another world snorkelling with
tropical fish.

Freedom is being able to laugh at your own jokes,
even if no one else gets them.

Freedom is letting the music dance you.

Freedom is knowing there's so much love in the
world we'll never run out.

Freedom is feeling the heartbeat of a baby asleep on
your chest.

Freedom is lying in the sunshine, letting the warm
rays caress your body.

Freedom is reaching for the stars.

Freedom is stroking a purring rescue cat.

Freedom is wearing red and purple and orange at the same time.

Freedom is jumping and splashing in puddles.

Freedom is what makes your heart sing.

Freedom is grabbing someone's hand and running too fast down a steep hill.

Freedom is not having a care in the world.

Freedom is smelling the green forest and hugging a tree.

Freedom is having thoughts that make you smile.

Freedom is wild squirrels taking peanuts out of your hand.

Freedom is re-living old photos full of happy memories.

Freedom is having a big hug with a stranger.

Freedom is letting go of everything.

Freedom is just be-ing, as a human be-ing, not a human do-ing.

Freedom is making 'angels' while lying in the snow.

Freedom is savouring a delicious mug of hot dark velvety chocolate.

Freedom is lying in bed being woken by birdsong with sunlight streaming in through the curtains.

Freedom is belting out your favourite song of all time.

Freedom is wild birds eating crumbs from your hand.

Freedom is having a no-make-up day.

Freedom is shelter and warmth and food.

Freedom is having the time to stop and smell the
    roses.

Freedom is smiling in sunshine and laughing in the
    rain.

Freedom is something you give to yourself.

Freedom is being able to be you.

Freedom is knowing there is a solution to every prob-
    lem.

Freedom is knowing there is enough.

Freedom is knowing I am enough.

Freedom is deciding to be happy.

Freedom is having no 'must', 'should' or 'ought'.

Freedom is being unconditional love.

Freedom is not having to look at your mobile every 5
    minutes.

Freedom is the sound of children laughing.

Freedom is getting lost in the moment.

Freedom is following your heart.

Freedom is resting in the wings of an angel, encom-
    passed in her love and protection.

Freedom is living in divine love and light.

Freedom is precious.

Freedom is everything.

Tricia Angelstar Davey, 70

17

Rhyme for Our Times

Our liberty has been taken away
People are turning on each other in hate
In the data we're afraid of, mistakes have been made
Our freedom is not theirs to take.

They all had underlying conditions
Giving a false cause of death was commissioned
So they could take our freedom with our permission
We have all been wrongfully imprisoned.
What has happened to our innate wisdom?
This is authoritarianism.

These ridiculous rules that are being told
The oppressive laws that now unfold
To stop us catching the flu, they have no role
It's a ruse, there's no truth, it's all for control.

He said that a stitch in time saves nine
That if we fail to comply, we will be fined.
Being fined for having our own minds
No more hugs or love or being kind.

Barriers, screens and fear to divide
Isolated and alone, at home, confined.

Their propaganda manufactured our fear
They made us think that it was our idea.
What about the 300 nurses who didn't hear the
    cheers
Because they ended their lives in the last seven
    years?

And all the unappreciated key workers
Who were made to go to work
Where they're not respected or paid their worth
Because, without them, we would all feed the worms.

For the minimum wage slaves, struggling to get by
For everyone who's too tired to question why
For every person contemplating suicide
It is about time that we unite against lies.

If you think these vile dictators are justified
That your compliance is saving lives
This would be the time to open your eyes.
Stop and ask why, just like a child.
I have no desire to patronise
Just duck duck go your human rights.

They have threatened us with the military

Just like what happened with the Chinese
When they stood up to the tyranny
Now this dystopia's enforced globally.

There is no need to listen to me
If you turn that nonsense off of your TV
Ask yourself what it is that you believe
And whether you're even remotely free.

Now we're looking at forced vaccinations
Forget the testing and safety regulations
Better stop the vacations around the nations
Claim there will be mayhem if we don't obey them.

So many have needed medical access
Wrongly turned away, now they lay to rest.
We are all being controlled and oppressed with
    threats
As the lies unfold, we need to unite and protest.

A small group of puppets who we know are bent
Manipulate and lie for our consent.
But we can be wise to their torment
We are the 99 percent!

War is peace, freedom is slavery, ignorance is
    strength

Have we really got to a stage where we all just re-
    lent?
This is not 1984, the lies are disguised no more
We could all barricade our doors
Or...

We could all unite and stand up
Against the condemnation of free will and love.

Wise Wild Child

18

Out of Winter Comes Spring

For many days, I, oh, was so alone
No where to turn, scared to the bone.
I sat in my room, my addiction my answer
Yet, all it did was act like a cancer.
Eating away, at all that was me
For ever in this dark, I would never be free.
Day by day, more and more of me was lost
Winter kept on coming, covering me in frost.
It started off as a warm spring night
Little did I know so much cold was in sight.
In what felt like hours, but maybe just minutes
My very soul pushed to its limits.
My clothes stripped, my dignity too
That night I thought, I wouldn't see it through.
I lay there after, for what seemed like hours
Imagining on my grave, what type of flowers.
This my story, I told too late
And by that time addiction seemed my fate.
Winter felt like it would last forever
Never would I see my happily ever after.
I still feel lost but I've now got some light

Please, please realise it's not just your fight.

Open up and don't be afraid

Come in to the light and out of shade!

It won't be easy I can promise that

But what of you they took, is not all you're about!

You're here today, maybe not standing tall

But today can be the day you less and less fall.

Start your life and begin to remember

A time when the sun shone ever so bright

A time when you weren't alone to face the fight.

Draw strength from the fear and use it for power

And move away from your darkest hour.

As spring begins you start to thaw

Your days become less about fighting this war.

Your life is your own, not those little shites

Your life is your story, your publishing rights.

Kevin Bleasdale, 39

19

Something Has Changed

It was something to do with the eyes, I thought, something was different about the eyes. I couldn't tell what it was, but I knew it was there: a slight, subtle, difference. 'Don't be silly,' said Jess, my wife. 'It's your imagination. You've been tired lately, you need rest.' But it wasn't that. Yes, I had been tired, but I knew it wasn't that. There was something different. Something had changed.

It began with the face masks – I thought they looked strange at first – and then came the face shields which looked even more bizarre. But it was odd how quickly they became normal, just accepted, as though there was nothing unusual about wearing them at all. My workplace went from a happy, friendly place to one of mistrust and suspicion overnight. Soon, I was wearing one too, although I didn't know why. How will these protect us from whatever the problem is, and will they even make a difference? I thought to myself. No one had really explained what the problem even was, it was all very confusing. 'It'll be alright,' said Jess. 'Just go along to get along. Everyone's doing it.' And so I did, and before long it seemed normal to me too.

Each week brought something new, something which would help keep us safe, they said, but I wasn't sure. We had to have our temperature checked each time we entered the building at work. 'Whatever for?' I asked. 'To keep everyone safe,' came the reply. 'But I'm not ill,' I said. 'No, but you're safe,' they responded, smiling. Always smiling. At home I complained to Jess, the only one who listened any more. Everyone at the office just seemed to get on with it. 'Don't worry', she said. 'It won't be for much longer. We'll be back to normal soon. That's what they're saying, anyway.' It may be what they're saying, I thought. But it's not what I'm seeing.

Soon enough, they began testing employees at the office. 'Mandatory testing Facility' read the sign on the door. 'What's all this?' I asked, surprised. I didn't like the look of the test contraption, and the thought of it going up my nose even less. 'It's just to keep everyone safe,' came the reply. 'But safe from what?' I asked. 'I'm not ill.' But the man only smiled. I think it was here that I first noticed it. Something around the eyes, as he smiled up at me, but I couldn't say for sure what it was. There was something unusual about his eyes. And now that I thought about it, who were the people administering the tests? The same ones who had taken our temperature upon entering the building, and handed out masks and face shields, months before. When had they appeared? It seemed like they were part of the furniture now, but no one could remember when they'd arrived. 'It must have been just after the incident began', said Jess. 'They're only doing their jobs. Just keeping people safe. Don't worry about it. Things are getting better they say.' But if that was true, why did we need all these measures, I wondered. And what was it about their eyes? I couldn't put my finger on it.

Not long after, it was announced that a cure had been developed. The best scientific minds in the country had been working on it and finally it was here. But if things had been getting better, I wondered, why did we need a cure? Wasn't it going away by itself, whatever it was? But they had an answer for this too, as they always did. 'The cure was to prevent the problem ever occurring again,' they said. But I had misgivings. It didn't add up, I thought to myself. Jess, reassuring as ever, said 'I shouldn't worry'. 'The cure would make us immune, and we wouldn't have to endure the crisis ever again. When we are called, we should do our duty and take the cure,' she said. But I was nervous, and I didn't know why.

One day, as I walked my usual route to work, I saw queues of people all lining up to get the miracle cure. They all seemed happy to be in the line. 'It'll all be over soon enough,' I heard them say. 'Yes, this will fix the problem,' said others. But I was cautious. I wondered how something so important could have been developed so fast. Surely it should take years to create a thing like this? Why hadn't cures been developed for other illnesses so quickly? Things that had affected people for decades? I was suspicious of the cure, and a little afraid of it. The next person in line moved forward and there, standing in the doorway, was a smiling man who stared at me as I passed, the slight, but undeniable difference in his eyes.

I refused to join the queues when my call came. I cannot say why. Perhaps I am mistaken, but I see that odd glint in people's eyes a lot more now, both at work and in the street. The ones in the queues don't have it, but then later I see them again and it's there I'm certain. I'm not sure what it is. Today though, I went to the office and there was a new sign on the door at the entrance: 'Mandatory Vaccinations. No Jab, No Work!' Behind the door stood a smiling man beckoning me to enter. I pretended I hadn't seen him, as I slowly backed away from that building which had changed so much in so little time. Even the windows seemed to glint now, as though watching as I walked quickly away.

I ran home to Jess, and called her as I moved swiftly through the rooms, desperately hoping she hadn't left yet, as today she'd received her call too. I sighed with relief when she emerged into the hallway and hugged her tightly. 'Jess!' I exclaimed. 'Thank God! I thought I was too late.' And I pulled away looking into her beautiful blue eyes. 'What's wrong, silly?' she said, 'You worry too much.' And my heart sank as I saw it there, moving against the blue ocean of her gaze. Something glinting far away, calling for me to join it as Jess stood smiling up at me.

'You, you've taken it?' I stammered, shocked.

'Yes, of course I have. And you must too.' She said, that odd glint shining as she spoke.

'But why Jess?' I managed, 'Why?'

'Because it's freedom, of course. Real, pure freedom.' And she moved towards me, smiling.

I stumbled backwards, reaching for the door handle and opened it, desperate to get away, but there in the doorway was the smiling man from the office blocking my escape.

I don't remember what happened next. All I know is that Jess was right. I know freedom now. Pure, true freedom. I do not have to think for myself any longer. Something else does that for me now. And I worry a lot less these days, and smile a lot more. I'm smiling now in fact as I usher queues of people through the door.

Soon they'll be smiling too...

Stephen James Gray

20

Corona

Corona for the better

Or the worse?

I can't tell.

Loving the house where I currently live

It has the same name

As if it were part of the game.

Coincidence or fate?

It's time to love, not hate.

The virus lockdown

Still messing with me.

Making me feel depressed

And unfree.

Is it real at all?

But there are chances

To do things, like dances.

To travel, instead of far

To close places, with or without car.

This is the day

I might once say

That brought some peace

For my soul, a warm fleece.

Maria

21

Lament for Freedom

I sat again at the window
On yet another afternoon, face cupped in my hands
Thoughts of deepest gloom, pondering the why, the
        wherefores
For our ongoing loss of freedoms.

To see the empty spaces, to see the vacant faces
Where to go, who to see?
Houses of friends and family, now all barred to me.
No 'busyness' in the streets, shuttered shops
Empty cafes, deserted of chatter, exchanging views
About the things that matter.

What matters more than loading cases into a car
And heading off up north
To a cottage on the coast
Backed by views of mountains
And miles of open sky?

What matters more than being free to make these
        choices?

Different ways to brighten days – not exotic, not
     chaotic
No continental travel – just getting out, being free
From all the enforced tyranny.

It has lasted long this loss, over which some are too
     keen to gloss –
'Your desire to be free will be the very death of me
There's a virus on the move... more variants than be-
     fore!'
It has ground the spirits down
It has eviscerated hope, to the extent that many can-
     not cope
'Tis truly a slippery slope, and the collateral damage
     is no joke.

Mental health is part of the nation's wealth
Stolen from young and old, none of it by stealth.
The rules and regulations are backed by 'the science'
No room for manoeuvre, no dramatic licence.
Play your parts, don't be upstarts
Don't 'upset the apple cart'... just obey, or you will
     have to pay.

Tomorrow, I know I'll be back behind my window, ru-
     minating always
The rationale, the reasons for the incalculable loss of
     freedoms.

Marronica

22

How Much More Will They Take?

How much more will they take?

Fasten your seatbelt

Stop smoking

Stop adding salt

Stop eating fat

Stop eating sugar

Stop eating meat

Stop driving petrol

Stop driving diesel

Stay out of the bus lanes

We are watching

We can fine you

Stop using cash

Stop saying things we don't like

Stop 'liking' things we don't approve

We are watching

We can arrest you

Take the knee

Take down your statues

Denounce your history

Denounce your gender

Denounce your race

Denounce your religion

Wear a mask

Do not go out

Do not see your family

Do not see your friends

Do not shop together

Download our app

Track and trace

Snitch on your neighbour

Do not protest

Remove your children from school

Wear your mask!

Do not see your doctor

Do not see your dentist

Save the NHS

Stay home

Watch our daily briefings

Be afraid, be afraid, be afraid

You are infectious

Your breath is murder

Wear your mask!

You say nothing

Still you say nothing

You do nothing

Still you do nothing

You say 'more'

And you say 'close the nurseries'

You say 'refuse them treatment'

And you say 'refuse them freedom'

You stand by and watch

You are not there for them

You are not inconvenienced

You are working-from-home-happy

You have your salary

You have your nice house

You have your pension

You wear your mask

You virtue signal

You denounce the anti-maskers

You denounce the lockdown sceptics

You denounce the vaccine questioners

You switch on the BBC

You watch the master's voice

Promoting fear and hysteria

You embrace the national hypochondria

The uneducated children

The frightened children, the neglected children

The lost businesses

The suicides, the bankruptcies

The job losses, the depression

The lonely deaths, the 'other' deaths

You are not there for them

But little by little

You will become them

And they will not be there for you

Care

Now

Use your power

Stop the lockdown madness

Before there's blood on your hands!

Andrea Salford, 58

23

The Miracle of Matchstick

'Don't do it, Lucy,' said Matchstick in a soft voice. Lucy, sitting hunched over her kitchen table, started violently at the sound. Her heart flew into her mouth and her chair banged noisily to the floor as she shot from it, slamming her back against the kitchen wall, arms splayed at each side with hands icy, fingers rigid. She was alone and instantly terrified – where had the voice come from?!

The box of matches she'd been listlessly playing with on her kitchen table was open and empty, its contents scattered across the table's surface. Now, though, one of the matches was somehow standing upright of its own accord and looking straight at her!

'Don't be afraid, Lucy' said Matchstick kindly. 'You're not going insane and I've been given this opportunity to help you at the lowest point in your life... it isn't your time to go.'

Although still terrified, despite herself, Lucy was strangely reassured by Matchstick's soft, kindly tone. 'Wh-wh-who are you, and wh-why are you here?' she managed to stammer.

'My name's Matchstick and I'm here to stop you doing

what you intended to do,' he said, matter-of-factly.

'How c-could you possibly know what I was going to do?', stuttered Lucy.

'Lucy... you lost your temporary work due to current restrictions, you're not receiving money or help from anywhere, you've exhausted your savings, you've scant food supplies, your rent's overdue, your bills are unpaid, you haven't seen another soul in four weeks and you can't see any other way out of this hellish imprisonment than to put a permanent end to all of your pain... today. Now, did I miss anything?'

Lucy rubbed her eyes, opened them and shot a quick glance at her far higher than usual daily medication stack. She then redirected her stare toward Matchstick. He remained in the same position, as if awaiting her response. Irrationally, her fear began to subside in the face of this surreal apparition. Her heart had stopped pounding so hard it had hurt and she was no longer rigid with fear. Matchstick's presence was calm and reassuring [was she really assessing the demeanour of a matchstick, she briefly reflected], to the point where, with her unblinking eyes still fixed on him, she slowly slid down to retrieve the upended chair, righted it, and sat down on it to face him.

Matchstick was clearly gratified by this development. 'Ah, that's better. This situation isn't normal, I'll grant you that, but your initial understandable fear and incredulity's subsiding and you're now willing to suspend your disbelief in a talking matchstick. Brilliant! So, let's begin.'

'Lucy, your circumstances have brought you to over-whelming depression, despair and desperation. I'm here to tell you, though, that life rarely goes smoothly for any length of time without something happening to upset it. Sometimes something BIG causes this, sometimes some-thing small, and at other times it can be the 'daily grind' spiralling out of control that leads to deep suffering and anguish. What you need to know, though, is that when smooth life experiences collide with harsh, rough ones, it creates an opportunity for *real* change and transformation to occur, however discordant, damaging and painful this may seem for the collision's duration. Is this making sense so far?'

Lucy, lingeringly disorientated that she was conversing with a matchstick, considered her response and said: 'How does this apply to me? Can you give me an example?'

'Gladly,' said Matchstick.

'Consider the match box you were absent-mindedly playing with, just before I volunteered to become Match-stick with a capital "M".' 'You volunteered for this?', inter-jected a startled Lucy. 'Yes, willingly. Shortly, it'll become clear as to why.'

Lucy sat back, focusing intently on Matchstick as he proceeded.

'Consider a standard matchbox and its contents. Out-wardly, it comprises a cardboard sleeve with a sandpaper strip on one side. Inside, there's a cardboard box that holds a quantity of us matchsticks. We're made of wood with a smooth sulphur tip. All of us elements, of ourselves, are inert. We can do nothing alone and apart, *but* the potential for endless possibilities opens up when we unite! Picture it: the smooth tip of a matchstick, grating harshly and discordantly across a matchbox's sandpaper strip ignites a living, vibrant, dancing *flame!* Do you know just how many things can happen when light and fire spring into life, into existence?' Lucy opened her mouth to respond, but Matchstick was in full enthusiastic stride. 'I'll tell you – there's *no* limit to what they can help humans to achieve! Lucy, there's no limit to what they can help *you* to achieve... [incidentally, do you know your name means "light"? That was no coincidence, by the way.]'

Surrounded by deepening twilight, Lucy felt the first pang of a nascent hope that there might indeed be light at the end of a very long, deep and dark tunnel. Impulsively she sprang forward, scooped up Matchstick, struck his sulphur tip against the matchbox's sandpaper strip and with his dying breath he whispered, faintly: 'I willingly volunteered for this sacrifice, my death is the price for your life as you wouldn't otherwise have picked up and lit a match, and light and warmth *had* to enter your darkness. When I'm recycled, I'll live again and be able to help others.' In Matchstick's dying light, Lucy noticed through the tears springing to her eyes a leaflet pushed through her letterbox that she'd barely heeded. She caught the words 'phone buddies – help if you need it', just before Matchstick's flickering light died...

Still seated, Lucy became aware it was now dark. With one hand she dabbed a tissue on her tear-filled eyes and with the other, Lucy slowly stretched to switch on an electric light while looking with new sight at the leaflet with its offers of help. Through Matchstick's sacrifice, Lucy realised she'd been given a unique, inestimable gift of light and hope in the midst of overwhelming darkness – just enough, a pinpoint of light to enable the potential for hitherto unsuspected possibilities to enter her consciousness. Lucy gently picked up Matchstick's spent, fragile body and hesitated. She wrestled with an overwhelming desire to keep him, a powerful memento of a deeply profound spiritual experience, but realised this wasn't permissible – hadn't Matchstick said that sacrificing himself for her sake was the way for new life, new opportunities to occur?

Reluctantly, with a considerable wrench, Lucy carefully shrouded Matchstick's body in a fresh white tissue and gently placed him in the empty matchbox. She then reverently, with heartfelt gratitude, bore him to recycling.

Matchstick had made Lucy aware that she needed to release the past in order to go forward with light steps and a new-found trust in endless potential, via the small beginning of accepting an offer of help. While musing over this, Lucy's eyes fell upon the previously unheeded but now noticeably colourful eggs, fluffy chicks and bright daffodils border of the leaflet she'd initially ignored. It was Easter! Lucy wasn't yet aware of it, but another precious miracle of resurrection of hope with a promise of new life and previously unknown spiritual freedom in the midst of darkest desolation had occurred.

Claire B McGrath

24

Freedom When?

Flatten the curve, don't lose your nerve, but here we
  will still are
Locked in our homes, no freedom to roam or bending
  the bar.
Our life has changed, but not for the best, twists and
  turns have rustled the nest.
We are divided, two worlds have collided, causing
  conflict and deep-seated unrest.
'I want out! ' some cry, while others cave in, or
  simply comply.
But more lives are at stake if we carry on living a lie.
United we stand, stronger together, safety in num-
  bers, but when?
If we bow down, our freedom will fall and where are
  we then?
Let's rise up, take back what is ours without looking
  back
Or shrivel to dust, give all of our trust in those who
  attack.
One life, they say, let's live it and let's do it now
We can and we will because we know how.

Karen Smith, 57

25

Don't Take Us Down This Road

Don't take us down this road
Be careful what you do
Don't take us down this road
We will not follow you
To a cursed place where darkness lasts
For ever
And where the human race can never be together.
You have filled us with fear
And turned one brother against another.

We are the brokenhearted
Who never said goodbye
To those from whom we're parted
Left alone to die
'Cos you told a lie about death round every corner.
So a mother dies and she doesn't see her daughter
For the very last time
And her hand is held by no one.

You said that all the changes
Were meant to keep us safe

Then you put kids in cages

And we lost our faith.

We didn't vote for you to put bars on all the windows

Now you hide the truth and you watch us as the fear
grows

Till we're pleading with you

For the needle to be revealed.

Don't take us down this road

A foolish thing to do

Don't take us down this road

Is our advice to you.

You are making rules that are crimes against the
people

And what you've done in schools is a special kind of
evil.

We want freedom again

And you must give it or we will take it.

We want freedom again

And you must give it or we will take it

And you must give it or we will take it.

Gino Trigginai

[You can listen to the sung version here:
soundcloud.com/ginotriggiani/dont-take-us-
down-this-road]

26

Time to Swim

Thinking, thinking of what to do
Time for a job? Or just something new?
As years have gone by and though things seem good
My mind's in a place wondering, if I should.
Should I be ready? Time to get on
Rebuild my life, now the world's moving on.
Lockdowns ending, my sanctuary expiring
Is it time to look for someone who's hiring?
In this new world I need to find purpose
Now my life is no longer a circus.
The future's a blank canvass and I'm the artist
Even though, I've never been the smartest.
But I want to succeed and make myself proud
Move on from the past and shine out loud.

Kevin Bleasdale, 39

27

Crimes Against Humanity

With the one track diabolical narrative being forced upon us, this might wake one or two up – just a very slim hope as most are blind, deaf and stupid.

Before you blindly follow any more draconian rules, read this:

Why did a Cambridge PCR test study of 10,000 people show a hundred per cent of their positives to be false?

Why are there many videos of empty hospitals?

Why are the Nightingale facilities being silently dismantled and closed, when there was a big hoo-ha when they were going up? Isn't it fantastic that we don't need them or do they not want you to know that?

Why is there video after video of people pretending to administer vaccines?

Why does 2020 have the fourteenth highest overall world death toll in last thirty years?

Why are there not masses of homeless dying from it on the streets?

Why does hardly anybody know anyone who's died only from it as opposed to with it?

Why are any deaths being marked as covid up to 28

days after a positive test? Particularly, as we only have to isolate for 10–14 days after a test.

Why has it only taken the lives of 388 under 60s with no underlying conditions in the UK?

Why have the Government not banned toxin filled food, alcohol and cigarettes which kills a ridiculously far greater number of people with awful cancers and such, if they really care about health?

Asymptomatic transfer is now debunked, so why are we still using this data to enforce restrictions?

Why are we still using Neil Ferguson as our 'expert' advisor, when he's failed to correctly predict pandemic numbers for the past twenty years?

Why are people being sent text messages from NHS saying they've tested positive when they didn't even turn up to the test centre?

Why are we pushing a rushed vaccine from a criminal enterprise that has broken records for claims, for a virus that is affecting literally nobody? That our immune system is dealing with on its own in 99.8% of the case?

Why aren't we discussing healthy lifestyles, diets, vitamins C and D3 and zinc etc. that can tackle this?

Why is hydroxychloroquine being banned from shelves when it's been proven safe and effective against other conditions?

Why are we being assured this vaccine is safe when we have no proof? Same scenario with swine flu jab 1976. Thousands claimed damages, of what was before guaranteed to be safe.

Why are the police being told to act unlawfully in dealing with anti-lockdown protests? Yet leave BLM etc. alone?

Why are we only hearing one-sided arguments from 'experts'? No debates, no alternative perspectives being addressed by the media or government.

Why enforce lockdowns and masks when, by their own data, it's proven they don't work and potentially even cause more harm than good?

Where is the Government's impact assessment on lockdowns? In September, covid was the nineteenth highest cause of death. Nineteenth! Why are we not addressing the eighteen others before it?

Why are we not informed about how long to wear a mask for before it becomes contaminated, which in turn is causing health issues like bacterial pneumonia?

Why were deaths marked down as covid even though post mortems were not carried out?

Why are there not specific bins for contaminated masks if this was so dangerous?

Why are we told to use antibacterial sanitizer when you need anti-viral to kill a virus?

Where has the flu gone? Twenty thousand less deaths in 2020.

Where has pneumonia gone? Seventeen thousand less deaths in 2020.

Committee of ten thousand academics constantly ignored.

I know people that have tested both negative and positive on the same day; how is this possible?

Why do the Government and their officials keep breaking their own rules if they are certain of the severity of this virus?

In January 2018 there was a flu outbreak that saw a 42% increase in deaths, why were no restrictions implemented?

Why shut down hospitality industry when it's been proven to only account for 5% of cases?

How are there still unoccupied beds in hospitals, when they're at capacity every winter?

Why do they insist on focusing on cases rather than deaths?

Why did we see videos in January, February and March of people dropping dead in the streets of China?

In July you were three times more likely to die of flu and pneumonia than covid.

Why, when they have already been caught in August exaggerating death figures, do you not think they'd do it again?

Why do they only fact check covid related content on social media?

Why are they not comparing the rise in cases to the rise in tests administered?

Why does it need millions spent via SAGE and The Behavioural Insights teams to influence [brainwash] people's thinking?

Why does it need social media influencers to be paid by the Government to influence the masses?

Why does it need media celebrities like Paul McCartney and Ian Mc Kellen influencing public opinion?

Why does it require a 24/7 sales and marketing drive?

Why have billions been paid out in non-tendered covid contracts to parliamentary chums for things like PPE?

How do doctors and nurses have time in 'war zone' hospitals to rehearse Tik-Tok videos whilst cancer appointments are cancelled?

Why are all NHS workers gagged against speaking out against the one-track narrative, are not allowed to voice an opinion, and face the sack if they do so?

Why no mention of the well-documented Global Reset in the same breath when covid-19 is so blatantly and actually being used to usher in this New World Order the globalist elite are so pushing for [as detailed in Rockefeller Lockstep 2010, UN Agenda 21/30]?

Why no talk of the current huge shifts in wealth currently happening across the globe [trillions of pounds]?

Why are the globalist elite making billions more money where 'lesser' people are driven to despair?

Why is there blanket silence in the mainstream media about the biggest protests in Indian history with millions upon millions gathering in Delhi?

Why no word of Event201 – a huge exercise of a Pandemic just six months before the 'real' thing? Surely they would mention this and say 'don't worry, we have practised for this very scenario'.

How is it the very people who organized Event201 now have all the answers and are now making billions from the pandemic?

Time to wake up UK!

Rise up and take back your human rights and freedom!

Julian French, 63

28

It Is Time to Fight for Your Freedom

It is always the innocents who have to lose their
      lives, in the seen or the unseen battles.
It is always the innocents who are put on the front-
      line, to be sacrificed.
It is always the innocents who are guinea pigs, to be
      tested upon.

Some are old and frail
Many lonely and scared
Others helpless and frustrated.

All because a few are hungry for power.
All they desire is to control others.
All they care about is growing their empire.

They will never change for they are lost and have no
      desire to be found.
They come back again and again in different faces,
      different dresses.
Their fathers have been doing it and their children
      will be doing it.

Only when the innocents open their eyes
Only when the innocents listen to their souls
Only when the innocents rebel and rise, will there be
      a revolution, will there be a change.

If not this time, you will be in bondage forever
Their children, your children
You will leave a trail of slaves forever.

It is time to free your wings
Time to act for your liberty.
Time to fight for your freedom.

The biggest questions are...

Do you know you are enslaved?
Do you know you are tracked?
Do you know you are numbered?

Do you know you are in a war?
Do you know you are in a battle once again between
      light and dark?
Do you know truth seekers are being shamed once
      again?

Not the kind of war you have read about
Not the type you have heard from veterans

Not the ones you have seen in films.

It is a silent war
A psychological war
A technological war.

The infantry is chosen.
The commanders are chosen.
The weapons are chosen.

In their little power euphoria, they execute with zeal.
In their zombie state, they think they care.
In their fear, they do as they are told.

Do they know they are being exploited?
Do they know they have been brainwashed?
Do they know they have become slaves?

Do they know they bear the 'mark of the beast'?
Do they know they have sold their souls to the devil?
Do they know they are serving the dark?

Dear Souls...

Do you know who you are?
Do you know what you are doing?
Do you know what is happening to humanity?

It is time to wake up
To see what you cannot see with your eyes
To read beyond the lines.

It is time to wake up to the light
To see who is what
To know your own existence.

That you are a natural being
You are a free being
You are here to free yourself, your children and in
    that, you free humanity.

It is time to free your wings
Time to act for your liberty
Time to fight for your freedom.

Rajya Lovelife

29

Connect the Dots

I'm not sure what people who support lockdowns are expecting.

Isle of Man only ended lockdown because it has full-and-total control of who comes in, and who goes out. The narrative is being spun that lockdown only ends when there are zero cases – which we're expecting to achieve with a dodgy test?

Think about Western Australia and Victoria – one case and three cases found respectively – and their entire states have been plunged into yet another lockdown. If authorities cared even a jot about economic recovery, they'd have a balanced approach. But no, the goal is to stifle any economic stability, and ensure economic destruction in liberal democracies to pave way for a new hegemony and social control, all with the aid of technology (track and trace comes to mind).

Despite what the media say, flights are still coming in and going out of the UK, not to mention the continued stream of migrant boats on our shores. And just to show their gratitude, one group recently burnt down a barracks they were being housed in.

So, by the philosophy of lockdown champions, how exactly are we to control the virus, if we cannot control the people coming in and going out?

Is it until the entire population has taken a vaccine which is still in clinical trials? That we all submit to this gene therapy experiment? Which still allows you to both catch and transmit the virus?

Are we all to be suggestible and follow every command of our masters, who have abused us for so long? Are we to give up our right to agency and blindly trust the chattering classes of technocratic 'experts'?

And don't forget, whilst these totalitarian restrictions go on in the West, many countries around the world are continuing as normal and not experiencing some kind of Armageddon, which the multi-million pound advertising campaigns are pushing.

Maybe the NHS is failing because those in power have sold it off, piece-by-piece, over the last three decades? There are plenty of efficient health services in the West which aren't overwhelmed, but the restrictions continue.

Yet of course, 'save the NHS', blame the people. It's a perfect shift-the-blame, divide-and-conquer campaign against the people.

How selfish that after a year of near solitary confinement for millions, people want to take the risk and instead live their lives. Especially given the extremely low mortality rate.

Maybe your neighbours and friends who are struggling

don't wish to exist for the sake of existing in perpetuity, until the 'benevolent' powers-that-be allow us peasants to continue our lives?

And, upon returning to their 'new normal', we return to a true disaster. An eye-watering debt shackled to future generations, a ruined economy with small businesses in tatters and corporations in control, a government who – due to our acquiescence – now says what, how, and when we can do what we do in our lives.

Please, connect the dots.

I guess the year-long brow-beating, fear-inducing propaganda, divisive talk, lack of debate, and exploitation of 'Greater Good' rhetoric has really done a number on the British people.

We've lost our resolve, our will, our fight for that precious thing, more precious than life, our liberties and our rights.

Julian French, 63

30

At the Behest of Old Nick

Quell the hope, choke the joy
Fan the flames of fear
Invert the words, wash the minds
Govern what they hear.

Hide the smile, condemn the touch
Suppress autonomy
Clip the wings, shut the cage
Slowly turn the key.

Cleave all faith, instil distrust
Engineer division
Whilst making sure that they believe
It's always their decision.

Coerce, corrupt, censor, deceive
Control at any cost
Crush dissent and common sense
Assemble all the lost.

Beguile the blind, corral the herd

Lead them to the gate
Where I wait with bated breath
To take them to their fate.

In doing so, you've played your part
And served me in my goals
Of complete dominion
And a harvest of the souls.

Gregg Brown, 50

31

Remember

Do you think it is your task

To virtue-signal and wear a mask?

Then think it over twice or thrice

The government is rolling dice.

Or rather, there is an evil plan

Meticulously worked out by a clan.

The elite are sitting at the top

They brainwash people and reap the crop.

At first the lockdown was meant for short

But lasted longer than most would've thought.

Earlier on, masks sounded like a joke

Now they're worn by left, right, and the 'woke'.

Corona restrictions are constantly here

Controlling everything from toenails to beer

Thoughtfully regulated by nanny state.

In truth, corona is just a bait:

We'll soon be invited to get vaccines

Which will become compulsory [behind the scenes].

By now you must've heard of Bill Gates

He'd like to reduce world population, he states.

I wonder where he'd want to begin?

He doesn't regard jab victims as a sin.

His goal is to vaccinate us, seven billion

He's not even a doctor though, thanks a million!

Surveillance and total control

For the megalomaniac the ultimate goal.

It doesn't only happen in history

Track and Trace is the new story.

Whenever Boris, Whitty and Hancock appear on TV

Close your eyes and sing: Let it be ...

There aren't as many dying from corona as shown

The covid death toll is clearly overblown.

Having treatment denied there are now more

Cancer deaths and suicides than before.

Masks have become mandatory

Mankind wears them like in slavery.

What can you do against the evil plan?

Don't worry about the [not so deadly] virus from
Wuhan

Instead care for the freedom you're about to lose!

Will poverty soon limit food, clothes and shoes?

For the sake of our children and the future genera-
tion

Remember, there's nothing normal about masks, dis-
tancing and isolation.

Bernice

32

How the World Stood Still

One day the great leaders of the world, whom everyone trusted and looked up to, told the people: 'Today your life as you know it is over'. It's not safe to go outside anymore because there's a Big Bad Covid Virus 'out there' rampaging throughout the land that's out to get you. So all the little people stayed indoors, cowering with fear under their comfort blankets, too frightened to go outside in case the Big Bad Covid Monster got them. And all the fun and laughter and hugs in life were gone. As all the little people stayed at home in fear, fear, fear. And people that were already sick died because they were too frightened to go to hospitals, which were nearly empty, but the great leaders told them they were full of people that the Covid Monster had got. So people stayed at home worried about their parents and grandparents and all the friends they couldn't see anymore, too afraid of venturing out, believing the Big Bad Covid Monster was out there.

And everyone said: 'Oh dear, oh dear, oh dear!' Only a few of the little people could still work, only those considered 'the necessary ones' by the great leaders. And the little people grew poorer and poorer, but the great leaders grew richer and richer because they allowed themselves and their big companies to work.

Once a week the little people were allowed outside to clap and bang on saucepans with spoons to thank the doctors and nurses for still working, even though they had so few patients to treat, as patients were refused diagnoses, treatments, and operations and died, while the nursing professionals made dancing videos.

As the weeks grew into months, just a few questioned how dangerous this Covid Monster really was. The great leaders made up numbers and drew graphs and told the people all day long on TV and radio, 'Stay Home. Stay Safe. Stay Home. Save lives.' or the Covid Monster will get you. They talked about 'flattening an invisible curve' with no base line, and reducing 'R' numbers using unreliable and highly manipulative tests to 'prove' it. Even though cracks appeared in the reasoning behind it, all the people still obeyed their great leaders because they were on TV, so it must be true. But no one actually saw the Big Bad Covid Monster because it was invisible. But still the leaders generated so much fear as their slogans brainwashed the people, so they all stayed home, whilst their livelihoods fell apart.

Many lost their own homes, and the old and sick died alone. No one laughed or hugged or played, or went to the pub or watched or played sports, or visited friends and relatives, no one sang or danced together anymore, there was no more joy in life, only sighs of 'oh dear', because all the people were living in fear. Except the great leaders. They still went out in their big cars, travelling the land and visiting lovers in their big houses, and held meetings and went to hunting and birthday parties, and met in very large groups to eat in the posh restaurants none of the little people could afford to go to, and flew first class without needing to quarantine, and still carried on doing all the things the little people weren't allowed to do.

Even though the commands were just rules and guidelines, and not the law, the little people still obeyed them because they were afraid the Covid Monster would get them. Very few of the little people questioned the great leaders and things got worse and worse and worse, and they became more and more afraid as they all stayed home saying: 'Oh dear, oh dear, oh dear!' as their lives fell apart more and more as each day passed. The months turned into a year, and still the little people stayed locked in, locked in fear, saying: 'Oh dear!' More people died, locked-down inside, and many committed suicide. And people sighed and people cried, but very few questioned if the leaders lied.

The great leaders promised only one way out: a vaccine which would 'save' the little people from the Big Bad Covid Monster, however, they still had to 'Stay In To Stay Safe', and cover their faces, and keep apart, and not visit anyone else's home, and no meeting up in groups, and no sport and no live music or dancing. And all the little people felt helpless and powerless still living in fear of the

Big Bad Invisible Covid Monster, that could still 'get them' even after vaccination.

When the few that questioned spoke out and said: 'we should all just "go out"!', the rest of the little people didn't believe them and became angry because the few weren't as afraid as they were. So they turned on them, telling them how stupid and delusional they were because they didn't believe the Invisible Big Bad Covid Monster was out to get them, and even started blaming them for making the Big Bad Covid Monster's existence bigger and worse than ever! The few kept insisting, 'we should all stop being so afraid, and go out and get on with our lives', as they challenged the belief that the Big Bad Monster, really was that Big. Or that Bad. Or really a Monster at all.

They also suggested there was another reason why the great leaders wanted all the little people to imprison themselves ... but again, the majority of the little people didn't believe them and turned on them because that's not what they were told on TV. The great leaders continued telling the little people they'd all die if the Big Bad Covid Monster got them, and that the Covid Monster had already killed thousands of little people, and it was very dangerous to go out. The few that questioned researched and discovered that no more people had died that year than died every year, and that the great leaders were telling lies to keep the little people too afraid to go out. But the little people continued to turn on them saying they were mad and 'tin foil hat conspiracy theorists' and blindly refused to consider any evidence laid before them, because they only believed what they saw on TV. So they stayed living in fear, crying: 'Oh dear!' for over a year. That's how we've got here.

So what happens now?

Are you locked into this pandemic of fear? Are you going to let the fear of the Big Bad Covid Monster destroy you?

Or will our story end 'happily ever after' with everyone waking up with cries of: 'Enough of the lies! We're all going outside!' and stepping out of fear into the sunshine and freedom?

Well dear reader, that is entirely up to you!

Tricia Angelstar Davey, 70

33

Lock up Your Daughters, Lock up Your Sons

Lock up your daughters
Lock up your sons!
Stay home virtue signalling watching TV
And swallow whole the scare notes on the BBC.

Lock up your daughters,
Lock up your sons!
Stop getting haircuts and stop walking the dog.

Don't get complacent
Put back on your mask!
Not asking questions is your only task.

Lock up your daughters
Lock up your sons!
Hide behind the sofa
Till the vaccine has come

And if they free you
Who knows when?
Don't let them ever do this again.

John Henry, 26

[A sung version is on the YouTube channel 'John X Henry': https://youtu.be/GWlpCiyDarU]

34

Mind Machine

Living our lives in isolation
Gone the days we were as one
From the roots this separation
What's the human race become?

Gotta survive in a techno nation
Computer screens control our lives
We're calling out in desperation
As one more part of our psyche dies.

A picture of progress or prostitution?
Serve the master mind machine
Selling yourselves to institutions
Chasing someone else's dreams.

In this age of alienation
Consumer world of plastic smiles
Binary coded information
Your name and number's down
On the files.

Salena Shatki Radford, 56

*[Although I wrote this in 2005, it speaks of the present
day situation that we are all now confronted with.]*

Sidekick

Being alone has me writing this rhyme
No superhero sidekick, no partner-in-crime.
Days spent in isolation
Gives cause for hesitation
To open your door
To wanting much more.
A friend for life
Doesn't mean a wife
But your partner-in-crime
In which to do time.
I've spent the last years, thinking it was OK
That being on my own was the best possible way.
I've tried with friendships but they all feel the same
No one's ever really driving in the same line.
Things start out great then they learn about you
See your troubles as a burden rather than under-
     standing you.
All I ask is to try and get me
I'm not asking for someone to come and save me.

Kevin Bleasdale, 39

Your Money

Apparently there was something going around

We had to do a full lockdown.

Empty all the cities and the towns

We'll spaff your money up the wall!

Spend hundreds of millions on PPE

From Liz Truss's mate's Shell company.

Charged three quid each, when it should be 10p

We'll spaff your money up the wall!

Give a fortune to big pharma

Sell the vaccine, cause a drama.

Get some RNA from a Llama

We'll spaff your money up the wall!

Hydroxychloroquine works but it's only 50 pence

Too cheap for them to make any sense.

Let's use Remdesivir for extra expense

We'll spaff your money up the wall!

Spend billions on track and trace

For teams of people to stare into space.

If they're lucky they might find one case

We'll spaff your money up the wall!

Take people out of work, pay them furlough

Give them eighty percent of their normal dough.
I think they would rather let their businesses grow
We'll spaff your money up the wall!
Encourage millions to have a test
Anything to ensure keeping folk distressed.
Another pointless amount to invest
We'll spaff your money up the wall!
Advertise propaganda on TV
It didn't take much for them to agree
What we've had to endure on the BBC!
We'll spaff your money up the wall!
So the country is two trillion in debt
For something that was never a threat.
Look at the numbers and start to sweat
They've spaffed our money up the wall!

Mike Smelt, 48

37

The Meaning of Brainwashing

Year 2050. On planet Earth. In a little village called Layham in East England.

'Grandad, Grandad, where are you?' Little Charlie comes rushing in, just back from school.

'I'm here.'

Little 9-year-old Charlie rushes to Grandad who was in the back garden tending to his roses.

'My friend Jerry said we are being brainwashed in school. What does brainwash mean?'

'Aha!' said Grandad. 'That is a good word to learn. Let me tell you a story to help you understand.'

'Yay! I love your stories.'

'Now let's go inside, let me make myself a cup of tea, you can grab something to drink as well and we'll go sit down on the sofa by the fire.'

'This is a true story. 30 years ago, on this planet, there was a fierce outbreak, the governments told the people it was caused by a certain virus. Now before you ask... a virus is an extremely tiny life-form. It is a sub-microscopic infectious agent that replicates only inside the living cells of an organism. You can get infected by it and have all kinds of symptoms in your body like fever or cough, etc. as your body tries to fight it.

It was not just in this country. It was all over the planet. Most countries were locked down. We could not travel. We could not meet our loved ones. We could not hug our families and friends, for, we had to keep a safe distance from each other.

The government, the television kept telling us how deadly this virus was and if we didn't do as we were told, we would all catch it and die.

The majority of the population feared for their lives. So, they did as they were told. Wore masks, kept their distances and stayed at home.

But the situation did not get better. It got worse.

Some of us knew the truth. That it was not going away soon because there was an agenda. Now, before you ask me what an agenda is,' Grandad smiles at little Charlie, 'it is a secret aim or reason for doing something.'

'So, what was the agenda?' Charlie asked, 'and who's agenda was it?'

'I see you are getting excited. I will tell you all about it. The agenda belonged to a certain group of people who considered themselves to be the elites, to be better than most of the people on the planet. These elites were half-humans, half-reptiles, but they showed themselves as humans. They had acquired a lot of wealth through wrong means, through selling various products by creating a type of fear first, feeding that fear to the people, then, telling them that they had the cure and they had the product. So, people would go and buy from them. That's how they made a load of money.'

'But that's not right, is it Grandad?'

'No, it isn't right, but that's how people used to lie and sell products back in those days. Their plan was to take over the world, microchip humans so that we all became like robots that these few could control and we would have no freedom.'

'It sounds like the bad guys in the film I watched last night, Grandad. The baddies were trying to do exactly that, turn humans into robots and control them, but Iron Man came and saved the world!'

'Who saved your world, Grandad?'

'Us normal humans. As I said earlier, there were some of us who knew the truth. But the majority just followed orders and did what they were told to do. Don't go here, don't do that, the government gave guidelines regularly for people to follow. The majority of people did not question anything. They believed that the Government was good for them.'

'But, aren't they good, Grandad?'

'The government we have now is very different from the government we had back then, Charlie. The people who worked for the government were weak and therefore, those elites with the money controlled them.'

'It was exactly like that in the film, Grandad!'

'Yes. So, most people kept following the orders

without questioning. They could not see or know what was happening although the evidence was visible everywhere. When we tried to tell them, they wouldn't have it. This carried on for a long time; for three years. To us who could see, it was war, but a different type of war. It was a silent war that was visible only to a few of us. It was also very sad. As we saw families got divided because that was the plan of the elites, to weaken humanity, by splitting up people – families, friends, loved ones. Society was divided into believers and non-believers. The believers believed in whatever information that was fed to them, they believed in whatever remedy that was being given to them for the virus. They were so tired after the first year they no longer had any ability to question anymore. Whatever little ability they had; they had blocked themselves with their complete trust in the government, their stories and their remedies. We, non-believers became rebels. We became the revolutionaries to fight for our freedom, to have our lives back.'

'Yay! Grandad, you are a hero!'

'It wasn't easy. Millions of people lost their lives on this planet. Hundreds of thousands became robots, who could not function properly as the technology failed and ultimately also died. Many people lost their loved ones in a painful way. But we carried on fighting. The country was in turmoil. There were many lawsuits, there were many protests and finally, those people in the government got done for their crimes. They were sent to prison and then a new government emerged out of that, which was much more connected with the people, as governments were always intended to be, to work for the people.'

'So, the moral of the story is... even when we go through challenges, know that there is always something good out of it. For, without the pain we went through at the time, we wouldn't have overthrown the old system of governing, we wouldn't have come to a much better time for humanity restoring our freedom once again. Hence, every challenge is an opportunity for growth.

It took almost 10 years for people to realise that they were brainwashed all because they blindly believed, and that's what brainwashing is: washing out your ability to think clearly by feeding you with misinformation.

But you must not blame the people who try to brainwash you because you cannot be brainwashed if you do not allow them to. It is only when we do not question why or what is happening and blindly believe it to be true, that's when we get brainwashed. You must believe it only when you know it. True knowing comes from within and that starts by questioning. Only when you ask, can you find the answer.'

'Thank you, Grandad, I really enjoyed your story as usual and I shall not allow anyone to brainwash me.'

Rajya Lovelife

The Ice Cream Sundae

Happiness, do you remember that word
When joy and laughter were part of this world?
A Summer holiday, and an ice cream Sundae
Love and affection could be on display.
But tough times hit, like we never thought
Society stopped for the fear of being caught.
Taken by covid or dobbed to the police
For the last 12 months there's been no peace.
Loved ones lost, families kept apart
For the NHS we do our part.
Society divided in what to do
Should I take a vaccine or see it through?
Freedom of speech, gone out the door
A difference of opinion? This means war!
Only together can we all pull through
The needs of many don't outweigh the few.
We pray for and hope for a better day
For a summer holiday and an ice cream Sundae.

Kevin Bleasdale, 39

They Lied

They lied about their modelling

They lied about the deaths

They lied about immunity

They lied about the meds.

They lied about PPE contracts

They lied about shutting schools

They lied about pathology

They lied about the rules.

They lied about effects on cancer

They lied about Vitamin D

They lied about track and trace

They lied about its fee.

They lied about susceptibility

They lied about asymptomatic spread

They lied about false positives

They lied about hospital beds.

They lied about the cases

They lied about the second wave

They lied about hospitality

They lied about how to behave.

They lied about the testing

They lied about the forecasts

They lied about conflicts of interest

They lied about the masks.

They lied about the care homes

They lied about data seen

They lied about absolutely everything

Now they want us to trust them with the vaccine.

Mike Smelt, 48

40

My New Normal Is Freedom

In my 'new normal' the world is a very kind and compassionate place where everyone is valued for themselves and everyone is treated fairly with respect and people can hug freely. We'll all have the freedom to be happy, free from financial and housing worries. We'll celebrate each other's differences and encourage each other to fulfil our dreams, follow our hearts and to fulfil our soul/sole purpose in life. No one will even think about doing harm to anyone or anything else. We'll be free to express the joyfulness of our divinity and let the music of our dreams play throughout our lives, dancing physically, mentally, emotionally and spiritually, as our hearts take flight in the bliss of the moment experiencing our oneness with the Source of All Life.

Tricia Angelstar Davey, 70

41

The Covid Cunts of Cumshire

I really do not like you:
You governmental men;
If there's one thing that can tackle you
It's the person with the pen!

You spout lofty announcements
[To keep us all secure]
Whilst you sly our jobs from under us
With one aim, to keep us poor!

You 'demonstrate' covidity –
All your ignominious team:
Make out we're well-nigh dying
And our faces are all green!

Not green enough for you my friends
As you're slicing up our pie
As you profit from our losses
And send interest sky high!

You pile with debt our students

At their 'happy time of life!'
You lock them in a dungeon
You're so desperate for strife!

You see the children hungry
To laden up your larder
How many men have killed themselves?
How many babes without a father?

They turn, the wheels of government!
They turn the minds of men
They stretch the realms of reality
To a looming living hell!

There're demon soldiers everywhere
Out baying for your blood!
They're depriving you of oxygen
Like you're lumps of flotsam wood!

With their manufactured illness
From those manufactured minds
They have no sense of wellness
They won't listen to the chimes!

Of the clocks of all the heavens
Of the warnings of our Kings!
But once they've killed us all off
They can't pull our prison strings!

They want instead your servitude
With not a seat to sit on
With not a hope of anything
And not a pot to piss on!

The measure of covidity
Is the liar's tune a humming
As for Boris's cronies' ministry
They think they've seen us coming!

'Acting in line with evidence'
Is the claim of that brazen crew
While they count covids (in their eminence)
Figures pilfered from the normal flu!

The Covid Cunts of Cumshire
Closed up the hospitality industry
With false declarations of disease
Just to alter the course of destiny (and with ever so
    much majesty)!

They want us without money
They want us working free
To labour without recompense
This offence is aimed at you and me!

The governing tyrants of the New World Order

Act on the notion that the water is all theirs
They believe we have no natural right to water
If you think it's yours, my friend, you'd better say
    your prayers!

They set on us a virus
That world experts have proven manmade
The worldwide Global Agenda caused
This knowledge to be betrayed!

Ignoring the evidence
From our doctors and peers
They treat us like small children
Like we're wet behind the ears.

The government wants us cashless
So they can gather every crumb
To make sure we're all accountable
Or they'll shoot us with their gun [their 5G or injec-
    tions that'll do some more than stun!]

All this focus on mental awareness
Rammed [by the World Health Organization] down
    our throats
None of them ever care less
So long as they turn you into their patients!

Not just to blame you Boris, for what it's worth

With your guidelines and rules to follow
You're with a pompous set of errand boys
Played by psychopaths in the shadows!

All credit for your master-plan
It must have taken some thought
But your blundering actions and contradictory lines
Guarantee you to be caught!

You take away our human rights
And think that we don't know
But we know about our Bill of Health
And our English Common Law!

We know where this is all going
It's all about Global Control
But one thing you don't realise is
Your agenda will end in free fall!

You can mask, martyr and muzzle
And force men to obey
But at what cost to the individual
Where no-one will have any say?!

Our soldiers that fell in the trenches
They sacrificed life for your freedom!
The government sit in their benches
They annihilate all that was hard-won!

By blood and sweat and sacrifice
Our rights were honourably protected
It's time to sort men from those boys of vice
To make sure that they're not re-elected!

Our old soldiers sit in the cold now
With no money spared for their morrows
They're down at the Salvation Army
Awash in a river of sorrows!

Our parents are holed up in care homes
With only the media for 'friends'
We don't get to see or to hold them
As they're nearing to where their lives end!

So two birds can be killed without blinking
Once they're dead they're not owed any pensions
And the government gets rich [while they're
    winking!]
Of course this is what nobody mentions!

Old folk worked lifelong for this privilege
With their fingers all cut to the bone
To end in the midst of this sacrilege
And not having a place to call home!

Face the Tyrannical World Order

The World's People for oppressing
For all the lies and arrogance
And a crime that needs redressing!

The Covid Cunts of Cumshire
With their covid New World Order
They're bothered about nothing
Except that they get to vaccinate you!

They want us to beg for a vaccine
As if we're in need of a cure
If you want to know what's on the Health Scene
They're destroying the old, the sick and the poor!

We will breathe our fresh air ever after
We will live under beautiful skies
We will rise up together, they will capture us never
Those governing bell-ends despised!

Maria Barnard, 63

42

No More Death

A new political Facebook group headed by a Deputy Head teacher and Momentum member has demanded an end to all-cause deaths in the UK. The group, which is now over 10,000 strong since its launch just 8 weeks ago is gaining members at an exponential rate in the wake of the coronavirus crisis.

I met with leader Ponellope Foopa at her home in the Cotswolds, where she lives with her husband Sebastien, an 'ethical' hedge fund manager concentrating on cobalt mines in the Congo, with whom she has an open marriage. For safety I entered through her leafy, extensive back garden. After fully disinfecting two chairs with disposable covers, she placed them four metres apart so we could conduct the interview. The aroma of freshly baked sour-dough bread drifted from the Aga oven in her Island open-plan kitchen. She insisted we both wear full PPE for the in-terview including a full face shield and plastic gown. For extra safety she also put up a full perspex screen between us. She commented: 'People have been left in the dark about the shocking rate of death in this country. Six hun-dred thousand people die in the UK every year. Who knew this shocking statistic? I can place every one of them down to this uncaring government and putting profit before lives! It has to stop!' she said, before bursting into tears and starting to shake.

She continued, 'only last week my friend, Henrietta, lost her 96 year old grandma. She was such an active lady when she was younger, riding horses and living life to the full. She had been in a care home and been suffering from dementia for the last 8 years and also had full-term bowel cancer. The fact that we let her die is a disgrace. There is no doubt that if we put her on a ventilator and kept her on life support for a while she could have pulled through: just another example of this uncaring government and the evil in society. There was talk of her sniffling in the week leading up to her death. To think someone with a cold could have gone to a park, passed it on to someone else by not keeping their distance, then that person passing it on to their child, who passed it on to their mother who then could have spoken to a care worker who then passed it on to her grandma ...!'

Her group are demanding a full lockdown of society: all shops shutting, a permanent end to all hospitality, weddings and socialising of any kind, locking the gates of all parks and outdoor spaces and only allowing home schooling with private tutors wearing full PPE for the next 5 years. 'The risks are just too great' she said, 'We cannot carry on living our selfish lives whilst 600,000 people are needlessly dying!' Piers Morgan who is a supporter of the group commented on twitter: 'I demand a government minister come and explain this disgraceful situation on Good Morning Britain tomorrow: 600,000 people dead every year and people still going out enjoying the sunshine in the park. They are traitors to this nation!'

I challenged Ponellope as to whether she was trying to cheat nature and the fact that life itself is a terminal condition. At this she got immediately defensive, called me a far-right sympathiser who only cared about money, not lives, and also accused me of being a racist, sexist homophobe and told me to leave her premises. As I stood up and stepped forward she screamed at me for breaking 'social distancing' laws and called the local police on her cell phone. Within two minutes three police cars and a riot van arrived, whereupon the debussed police officers sprinted through the house, rugby-tackled me to the floor then stamped on my legs and put me in handcuffs. Luckily I had a spare £30 in my pocket and so managed to pay my fine and hobble back to my car.

Mike Smelt, 48

43

The Heroes Journey

Digital soldiers your time will come
The truth is your weapon, not a gun
Your light shines forth like the brightest sun
Your hearts and minds are second to none
You carry no banner nor bang a drum
Words are your weapon via fingers and thumb.

This war on humanity hasn't been fun
As Satan's sting has surely stung
Atrocities to children leave one numb
Words alone sound trite and dumb
We must free the babes from Satan's scrum.
Sacrificial innocence held in a DUMB*
No mercy or compassion not even a crumb.
Adrenochrome harvesting draconian
So demonic, its source is not human
Everything points to Draco-Reptilian.
The pain and trauma is too much for some.

But keyboard fighters don't succumb
This is it, there's no re-run

The battles are many but you're nearly done.
Now evil demons have nowhere to run
Exposure of fraud and lies has begun
Disclosure of truths will shock and stun
All crimes will be counted in Nuremberg's sum
All complicit collaborators both old and young.

Your heart and soul's mission is for freedom
Spiritual warrior, you know we're all one
Keep your vibes full of light for everyone
Love and Light's victory shall not be undone.

The Song of Awakening is being sung
3D to 5D has already begun
Ascending Jacob's ladder rung by rung.
DNA entwined in divine perfection
Holding the world in love's protection
Restored to your divine connection
Souls united in triumphant celebration.

Seeing through this dark illusion
Makes you part of the solution
Because of you this war will be won
In you I'm well pleased, my daughter, my son.

Tricia Angelstar Davey, 70

[DUMB is a Deep Underground Military Base]*

44

Goodbye Freedom

Goodbye freedom
It's been nice knowing you.
Police are now marching the streets
Soon there might be a curfew.

Goodbye freedom
We took you for granted, I guess
We're forced to wear masks
Seems people couldn't care less.

Goodbye freedom
Why don't people resist and rebel?
Instead, they're complying without doubts
Do they really want this hell?

Goodbye freedom
Freedom – what a great word!
Meaning free to go out and about –
Now freedom's gone, it's absurd.

Goodbye freedom

We'll meet again, I'm sure.

Nothing can separate us forever

Truth and love is the cure.

Bernice

45

Another Ode to Liberty

The well-spring of hope and triumph of life: freedom!

You call across the land even if unheard, still the earth and air reverberate with you. The voice of yours is light-ning and earthquake across the nation. You scorn chains. Though the dull smoke of tyranny that masks your sight grows thick over the dulled nation, still your passion and lustre are undefiled, unhidden, though the pen of the censor seeks each day where last you left your mark, and ex-tinguishes it with offended, tyrannical fury.

Like the chill of early winter, the chill of tyranny rolls on in the ineloquent vaunts of Boris, Biden's faceless stare, the calumny of parliament in their statuesque discourse of oppression abstracted from all life and passion, yet you, freedom, who wear no crown and do not noose the people with masks as if you were crowned thereby, still rage on in the flow of vitality and you create the spirit that drives art and passion and revives poetry, though Carol Ann Duffy had killed it and desecrated its corpse long ago.

Chains of the lockdown now have grown as whales into their kin. Censorship. Though at first the chains seemed small enough to most, yet soon innumerable chains suffused society and dampened its heart. Fear of the virus has become the mask for the fear of freedom, the fear of liveliness and of hope, and now society monitors itself, and each monitors themselves, and all are afraid of their own shadow.

Lizard-like, this tyrannical Jörmungandr circles round the world in its unbecoming coils. Their fear is such that each time a new panic begins, then freedom, branded anew with the names of evil and Satan by its detractors, is proclaimed enemy of all.

Freedom, that feels like fire in the souls of all who know it, moves them like a fire's motion spontaneous and untethered. Awake, it rises still, in awakening it naturally rises in defiance, and scorns the barren graves that the masked legions and parliament enter early, and make fortress as the world fades from their view.

For in the lockdown, men fall to vile obedience of the debased establishment, by their droves, and are trained to serve in this clampdown's unwelcome machine. The whale, and monster, dead tyranny, still ranges the land in rage, its hatred for the free now clear.

Yet freedom still declaims death's mask, to which woollen knees bow, and declaims the beast's mark they wear, and in freedom's splendour, its suffusion of a life more lively than life itself, dispels the evil eye the graven idols of death's worshippers cast when masked.

Freedom, hold us aloof from tyranny's monotone submission.

Evans Trump

46

Freedom Lost, Freedom Found

One day when I am old
And my children come to me
They'll ask a poignant question
When did the world stop being free?

'Mum, what were you doing
When the world was closing down?
Dad, did you stay silent
When they shut the shops in town?'

'Did you really clap on doorsteps
And for Captain Tom you cheered?
Did you give up Sunday worship
While our freedom disappeared?'

'Were you busy watching Netflix
While furlough drained the purse?
Did you order endless take-aways
And ignore the lockdown's curse?'

'Did you ever see a future

Like the one that we are in
When freedom for the masses
Is a memory, growing dim?'

'Mum, were you complicit?
It's a question I must ask.
Did you speak up or were silenced?
Were you muted by the masks?'

I will tell them of the struggle
To find truth where others lied
I will tell them how I spoke up
And share how hard I tried.

I will speak of propaganda
People blinded by their fear.
'I am sorry', I will tell them
'I watched freedom disappear'.

It was not for lack of trying
We fought with truth and fact
But the media played dirty
Used emotion to distract.

So we chose to step away
And not follow the advice
That's why we live in freedom
In our off-grid paradise.

Liberty Walker

47

The Free

I am the sun and all that shines
I am the clouds, the shapes, the lines.
I am the wind and all that blows
I am the trees, the food that grows.

You are the seas and all the waves
You are the storms, the mountains, the caves.
You are the love in every child
You are the light, the soul, the wild.

We are the Earth and all that flowers
We are the strength, the peaceful powers.
We are the courage, some disagree;
We are the few, the many – the free.

J. J. Ahern, 33

48

Young and Social

When do they get their social lives back?
It's critical they get them back on track.
The young need their friends, it's plain to see,
It's hard to find any that disagree.

The landlords need to open their pub,
Without a substantial meal, or dodgy grub.
What is the issue with going for a drink?
Forget the zealots creating an irrational stink.

Let the young ones have a rave,
It's pointless telling them how to behave
They are unaffected by this disease,
It is fought off with incredible ease.

Let them go out and dance in a club,
Whether it be house, or grime or dub.
They cannot be denied of living free lives
Or possibly meeting their future wives.

All this time without going on dates

Or meeting up and seeing their mates.

It simply cannot go on any longer,

Their feelings of isolation getting stronger.

Watching live music, going to gigs,

Rather than staying in solitary digs

It's simply unfair and completely pointless

Remembering the good times with increasing fond-
ness.

Travelling stopped, the missing gap year,

Meeting new friends over a beer.

None of this was necessary, it has to stop,

The challenge is convincing those at the top.

Mike Smelt, 48

49

Living Dead

Somewhere, in the deep recesses of my soul
There is a flame
Feeble and flickering reaching out to my heart.
But my sentient self struggles to find that spark so
        essential to me.
The hope, the optimism and the promise of the life I
        knew
So precious, so dear, so fragile, so easily blown apart.

The spark flickers and fades
Under a welter of dystopian masks
Fearful glances and glowering eyes.

Walk there, don't stand there
Go this way, go that way.
Who are you, why are you?
Don't smile, don't sing
Stay home, don't see anyone.

Do this, do that, don't do that
Don't breathe in, don't breathe out.

Sometimes I wish I didn't have a mind
Then I need not think for myself.

Sucking the life out of life
Crushing the comfort of camaraderie
I am a husk, a shell
A shadow of my former self.
As I live and breathe, I might as well be
The killer I am held up to be
As the spark stutters and dies
I become a zombie.

Alys Glass

50

In the Heart of an Englishman

What lies in the heart of an Englishman?
Behind that weathered edifice.
Hidden in gloomy moorland, and winter waves
Lapping forlornly on pebbled beaches
By squally rain that comes and goes, scattering
    crowds rushing to and fro.

All the while he stands solemnly, doing what he
    must.
Born to freedom but tied to tradition
Which not for any reason he grows to love.
No, reason that continental thing. That thing of busi-
    ness and science
Of travel and logic; but not for an Englishman.
Not for one who grows as the oak; is sheltered under
    Portland stone.
He never quite knows why, never can pin it down. It
    lives within him.

Often, he'll catch a glimpse, see a flash

And that grey heart, tempered by grey weather,
　　warms.
Hymns: melancholy, ancient rhythms, that in a mo-
　　ment give him pride.
Standing stock steady at evensong, singing without
　　care nor hindrance.

Evil is at work. Evil are those who shut the doors,
　　keep us apart
Tape up the pews, silence our voices.
As mendacious sages intrude, the Englishman's heart
　　churns and foams
Letting those buffeting waves, that lingering fog,
　　overwhelm him.

Edward Gifford

51

Fight for Our Freedom

Don't want a lockdown anymore
I want the life I had before.
Don't you remember being free?

'Cos now I hide behind my door
While they lie to me more and more.
I'm tired of this captivity.

So we must fight for our freedom
Because they can't take our freedom
How will we live without freedom?

And now the vaccines are in view
And they will test them out on you.
They've had some problems, did you know?

But you'll need one to circulate
Or you don't go past the garden gate
And there'll be nowhere you can go.

So, we must fight for our freedom

Because they can't take our freedom
How will we live without freedom?

I see a future full of masters and slaves
It's a world they'll build upon a million graves.
A million graves!

Now the plan is very clear
The world we know will disappear
We must let people know the truth!

'Cos they are going to instigate
The jackboot of the police state
And they will never turn us loose.

So we must fight for our freedom
Because they can't take our freedom
How will we live without freedom?

How will we live without freedom?

Gino Trigginai

*[You can listen to the sung version here: soundcloud.-
com/ginotriggiani/fight-for-our-freedom]*

52

Stand Together

Were we born to live our lives

Or live a lie until we die?

Hear what I say

We'll find a way.

Stand together, join our kingdom

Spread the word, we need our freedom.

Free to run, to spread our wings

Free to love... so many things.

Everyone should know what 'their' agenda holds

Time will tell as the future unfolds.

Don't be fooled, this is all a lie

To take control of you and I.

Do your research, don't be a sheep

You'll be trodden on while you're still asleep.

Act now, before it's too late

Spread the word, or face your fate.

Caroleann, 65

53

Back to School

Upon entering the gates, one is greeted by a swathe of over-precautious nonsense, that is if you don't have a muzzle upon your person, you will be greeted with a detention by a compliant teacher wearing a face rag. Dehumanising mask in hand, you will be directed to the allocated area for your year group, where you shall be named, counted and muzzle-checked in a process called 'roll-call'. Like the criminals we are, for having the audacity to receive an education.

After a questionably 'brief' lecture about how these ludicrous measures are supposedly 'keeping us safe' and making sure nobody dies from a disease that doesn't affect people our age in the slightest, we are made to cover our faces and are escorted to our room by a teacher. When entering and exiting every room, no matter how long we have been in there for, teachers stand over us glaring like hawks to make sure we get a large, unhealthy dollop of hand poison. The same applies every time someone coughs, sneezes accidentally, is polite enough to pick up someone's pen [the horror], or performs any other actions which may be christened 'cross-contamination'.

No equipment can be borrowed, for example: art supplies, glue sticks, whiteboard pens, calculators etc. making our schoolbags much heavier than they would otherwise be, and since lockers are no longer in use, we have to cart around lots of belongings. This includes drinking water, seeing as the water fountains are now off limits! When lessons finish we will either be escorted to our next class by a teacher or escorted to the car park where we have break or lunch wearing face 'protectors'. When lunch is upon us we do not have the luxury of having somewhere to sit, so instead we dine on the cold hard concrete unless we are willing to buy overpriced food for a seat indoors. At the end of lunch we are made to line up and once more muzzle up and then wait to be escorted to the next lesson of the day.

Our classrooms are always freezing because the windows and doors are always open for so-called ventilation. Another common feature of the classrooms is the yellow tape on the floor indicating the 'zone' that the teacher is not allowed to leave and we, the 'diseased students', are not allowed to enter. In fact most of the school and the sports changing rooms are shrouded in yellow tape. For example, the changing rooms are split into small yellow prison cubes that we have to get changed for PE in by ourselves. Excessive sanitisation is also common in PE like the hand poison we have to use and the bleaching of equipment, such as tennis balls before and after use.

A new rule has also taken effect: different coloured

lanyards are to be worn to make sure that you do not mix with other year groups and stray from your 'bubble'. Year group bubbles are a big issue because it means if one of your year group supposedly tests 'positive' your whole year group i.e. all 300 of you, have to stay off school, missing out on fundamental education for two weeks! The same thing has happened at our school for Year Eleven and because so many bed-wetters of parents of students from other year groups have taken their children out of school, leaving a partially empty building.

The pointless wearing of face coverings are more than irritating as it distorts your words, creates a sense of de-humanisation and lessens your oxygen supply all of which is of course not a good thing. One of my friends is forced to wear a face rag despite her father's e-mail to the school stating how the masks have caused a change in the child's breathing patterns.

Overall there have been many ludicrous new rules in-troduced to our school and in my opinion none of them do any good and this is the same with many schools across the country, therefore I would very much like to get back to normal and stop all this nonsensical madness.

The End

Macy, 13

Appendix

For more copies of this book, please visit:
thewhiterose.uk/book

Join the resistance and receive our newsletter:
thewhiterose.uk/newsletter

Lightning Source UK Ltd.
Milton Keynes UK
UKHW011434061221
395182UK00003B/793

9 798729 434770